MICHAEL JORDAN

Hall of Fame Basketball Superstar

Nathan
Aaseng

HALL
OF
FAME

SPORTS GREATS

Speeding Star
Keep Boys Reading!

Speeding Star, an imprint of Enslow Publishers, Inc.

Library of Congress Cataloging-in-Publication Data
Aaseng, Nathan.
 Michael Jordan : hall of fame basketball superstar / Nathan Aaseng.
   pages cm. — (Hall of fame sports greats)
  Previously titled: Sports great Michael Jordan
  Includes bibliographical references and index.
  Summary: "Learn about Hall of Fame basketball player Michael Jordan in this sports biography. See how Michael became arguably the best basketball player ever and changed the Chicago Bulls organization forever. Read about how he even retired from basketball to play baseball!"—Provided by publisher.
  ISBN 978-1-62285-035-8
 1. Jordan, Michael, 1963- —Juvenile literature. 2. Basketball players—United States—Biography—Juvenile literature. 3. Chicago Bulls (Basketball team)—Juvenile literature. I. Title.
  GV884.J67A26 2013
  796.323092--dc23
  [B]
                            2012050554

Future Editions:
Paperback ISBN: 978-1-62285-036-5   EPUB ISBN: 978-1-62285-038-9
Single-User PDF ISBN: 978-1-62285-039-6   Multi-User PDF ISBN: 978-1-62285-150-8

Printed in the United States of America
042014 Lake Book Manufacturing, Inc., Melrose Park, IL
10 9 8 7 6 5 4 3 2

To Our Readers: We have done our best to make sure all Internet addresses in this book were active and appropriate when we went to press. However, the author and the Publisher have no control over, and assume no liability for, the material available on those Internet sites or on other Web sites they may link to. Any comments or suggestions can be sent by e-mail to comments@speedingstar.com or to the following address:

Speeding Star
Box 398, 40 Industrial Road
Berkeley Heights, NJ 07922
USA

www.speedingstar.com

Photo Credits: AP Images, pp. 15, 18, 23; AP Images/Alex Brandon, pp. 1, 29; AP Images/Brian Cleary, p. 5; AP Images/Jack Smith, p. 59; AP Images/John Swart, pp. 31, 34, 40; AP Images/Mark Duncan, p. 45; AP Images/Michael Conroy, p. 13; AP Images/Michael S. Green, p. 55; AP Images/Reed Saxon, p. 37; AP Images/Robert Kozloff, p. 43; AP Images/Stephan Savoia, p. 60; AP Images/Ted S. Warren, p. 26; AP Images/Tim Boyle, p. 11; AP Images/Wayne Fleisher, p. 51.

Cover Photo: AP Images/Alex Brandon

This title was originally published in 1997 as *Sports Great Michael Jordan, Revised Edition*

CONTENTS

A Score to Settle

Chicago Bulls fans smugly inched forward to the edge of their seats. The twenty-four-second shot clock had been turned off. In just a few ticks of the clock the fans would leap in celebration of another sweet playoff victory.

True, the Bulls led the Orlando Magic by only a single point. However, the basketball was safely cradled in the hands of Michael Jordan. "His Airness," as sportswriters called him, was simply the best basketball player in the world. He had been away from the court for over a year, and the Bulls had suffered. Now he was back and there was no way the Bulls could lose.

Yet as Jordan dribbled up the court, the Magic's Nick Anderson silently swooped in from behind. Before Jordan

Ball in hand, Michael Jordan dribbles up the court. Moments later, Nick Anderson of the Orlando Magic swooped in and stole the ball.

could react, Anderson reached in and tipped the ball. It bounced away from Jordan. Orlando's Penny Hardaway chased it down and threw a pass to Horace Grant who raced unguarded to the basket. Grant slammed home the ball for the winning points of the game.

The basketball world looked on, stunned. Michael Jordan stripped clean like a rookie? Michael Jordan lost the ball and gave away the game? It was like watching a world-class gymnast fall flat on his face in a championship meet. Chicago's star added to the nightmare by passing up a last-second crucial shot, and instead, throwing a bad pass, which sealed Orlando's victory.

Jordan shook off the humiliation to pour in 38 and 40 points in the Bulls' next two playoff games against Orlando. Yet the Magic outplayed the Bulls and took the series lead, three games to two. Facing elimination on their home court, the Bulls battled back. They pulled ahead comfortably in Game 6, 102–94, with just a few minutes to play. Again, the game seemed as good as over.

Incredibly, Orlando's shooters went on a tear while Jordan and his mates fell apart. The Magic whittled down the Bulls' lead and then actually pulled ahead. It was time for Jordan to answer with one of the miracle shots or impossible, twisting drives for which he was famous. Jordan launched a long shot . . . and missed not only the net, but the rim. He drove to the basket . . . and instead of soaring for a layup, threw a bad pass to a teammate. Orlando scored the final 14 points of the game to win, 108–102. For the first time in four playoff seasons, Jordan walked to the locker room a loser.

A humble Michael Jordan sat in front of his locker, answering questions from the press. "I'm not going to sit here and try to make excuses," Jordan said. "Obviously, we're not the same team as eighteen months ago," when Jordan last played for the Bulls.

He did not add what many observers were saying—that Michael Jordan was not the same player as eighteen months ago. The man who had won many National Basketball Association (NBA) scoring championships, and the Most Valuable Player (MVP) in three straight NBA championship series, had come down to earth. Nick Anderson, who had stripped Jordan on that crucial play, came out and said the obvious. Jordan, said Anderson, was "not as sharp" as he used to be.

Scottie Pippen watched Jordan suffer through the post-game grilling after the loss. No one knew better than Pippen how fiercely competitive his teammate could be. Even at the height of his success, Jordan practiced with a burning desire that was sometimes scary to his teammates. He was a driven man who could not stand to lose a round of practice shots.

"Michael's not used to being in a position of talking about why we didn't win, and I'm sure he didn't like it," Pippen observed. Maybe Jordan no longer was invincible. Maybe he could no longer dominate the league and lead the Bulls to the title. Yet he would not give up without a fight. Pippen knew that the Michael Jordan who came back in the fall would be a man on a mission. And while Jordan on a normal day had often been spectacular, he had been out of this world when he had something to prove on a basketball court.

Just ask Larry Bird. In the summer of 1984, Jordan stepped on a court against the Boston Celtics superstar for the first time. Jordan, a junior at the University of North Carolina, was a member of the United States Olympic team. They were about to play a team of NBA players led by Bird.

During warm-ups before the game, a basketball got away from the Olympic players. It bounced toward Bird, who was shooting on the pros' side of the court. Jordan trotted over to fetch the ball. Bird picked it up. Jordan held out his hands for Bird to return the ball. Instead, Bird kicked it over Jordan's head. "He was showing me it was all business and I was beneath him," Jordan recalled. "I didn't forget."

From that point, Jordan was on a mission against Bird. He and his Olympic teammates beat the pros that day. Then, two years later, Jordan almost single-handedly took on Bird and the Celtics in a playoff game. Jordan slashed through and soared over basketball's best team for four periods. He fired long jump shots past Bird and Celtics ace defender Dennis Johnson. He spun the ball through the long arms of Boston's big men, Bill Walton, Robert Parish, and Kevin McHale. As time ran out, Jordan drew a foul and calmly sank two free throws to send the game into overtime.

Boston finally squeaked out a win—but not before Jordan scored 63 points, an NBA playoff record. The Celtics were shaken by Jordan's performance. "I thought he was awesome the last time we played him," said K. C. Jones. "I don't have a word for him this time around."

Jordan had settled his score with Bird. The Celtics forward now wondered aloud if Jordan was "God disguised as a basketball player." The message Jordan had delivered was clear: challenge Michael Jordan at your own risk.

Others had learned that lesson over the years. For several years, many "experts" claimed that Jordan was too selfish a player to win an NBA championship. Stepping up his play to uncharted levels, Jordan not only proved them wrong, but led his Bulls to three straight titles.

Now, after all that success, Jordan had not only lost, but had been embarrassed on the court. He had a score to settle. Scottie Pippen knew that the Bulls were in for an interesting year.

Chapter 2

High School Is Hard Work

Michael Jeffrey Jordan was born on February 17, 1963, in Brooklyn, New York. He was the fourth child and third son of James and Delores Jordan. Shortly after Michael's birth, the Jordans moved back to James's hometown of Wallace, North Carolina. There, one more girl was born into the family. When Michael was seven, the family moved just down the road to Wilmington, in the southeastern corner of North Carolina.

Michael has credited his parents with paving the way for everything he has accomplished. "From day one they taught me right from wrong," he said. His father showed him the value of hard work. James's steady effort helped him advance from mechanic to a plant supervisor with General Electric. Like her husband, Delores Jordan worked her way from a low-level position to supervisor at a local bank. She was the one most responsible for teaching Michael the value of discipline. Both parents kept after their children to study hard in school.

Michael's keen interest in young children may have been touched off by his own unfortunate childhood experiences. Other kids made fun of the way his large ears stuck out from his head. Michael grew up believing that he was ugly. As a result, he was shy and awkward in social groups and did not go out on dates in high school. Convinced that no girl would ever be attracted to him, he took courses in cooking and sewing to prepare for living alone.

Michael did have a gift for sports, however. His parents first noticed his exceptional skill at bouncing a ball when he was only two years old. For many years his best sport was baseball. Jordan could play any position. He could hit well and could fire his fastball past most batters. His most precious childhood memory was when his Babe Ruth team won the state championship with Jordan as the tournament's Most Valuable Player. James Jordan began to think that his boy might be talented enough to become a professional baseball player. A number of pro scouts suspected the same thing. Several of them kept a close eye on Jordan and his flaming fastball as he moved into high school.

Jordan's talent was not limited to baseball, however. Michael loved to compete in all sports, and he enjoyed the respect that he could earn with his talent. He played quarterback on the Laney High School football team in Wilmington in the fall of the year. Between baseball games he dabbled in the long and

Growing up, and even as a professional, James Jordan was a father and a friend to Michael. Jordan even picked up his father's habit of sticking out his tongue when he is very focused on something.

high jumps for the track team. Basketball was not his favorite activity. Still, as long as it was a sport, Michael would try it. He especially enjoyed creating his own acrobatic shots.

After he suffered an injury playing football, his mother urged him to think about giving up that sport. Michael listened to her and spent more of his energy on basketball.

Neither of Jordan's parents was unusually good at sports. The only technique that Michael patterned after his father was the way he stuck out his tongue when he played. James Jordan had a habit of sticking out his tongue when concentrating on any project, even one in his garage workshop. Little Michael copied the habit and has not been able to shake it to this day. Still, James Jordan encouraged his boys' interest in basketball by building them a full-sized court in their backyard. For instruction and competition, Michael relied on his older brother Larry. The two of them played together on their court nearly every day.

Michael Jordan may be the best basketball player in the world, but he has always considered himself the second-best player in the family. Larry, who is one year older than Michael, "always used to beat me in the backyard." It was Larry who taught Michael the free-wheeling, gambling, aggressive style of play that he has carried to the pros. Michael is convinced that it was only the breaks of nature that kept Larry from being the sports legend that Michael has become. He insists that Larry can jump higher and can perform all the moves that have made Michael famous. Larry's only fault was that he stopped growing at five-feet seven-inches.

Despite his great coordination, Michael Jordan was not an

Michael Jordan's brother, Larry, was the one who showed him many of his famous moves.

instant success on the basketball court. During his sophomore year, he could not make the starting squad at Laney High School. He sat, fuming, on the bench the entire season. The coaches seemed to pay attention only to how tall a player was. Jordan's best friend was six-feet six-inches tall, while Michael stood only five-feet eleven-inches. Even though Michael was certain that he was the better player, his friend played instead of him. Jordan was so bitter about being benched that he privately rooted against his team.

In 1979, between his sophomore and junior years, Michael grew four inches, to six-feet three-inches. That, plus a great deal of hard work, helped him to finally crack the starting lineup. For one season he got to play alongside brother Larry in the Laney backcourt. Michael thought so much of Larry that he chose to wear number 23 on his uniform. That was as close as he could get to one-half of Larry's number 45.

Jordan's hero as a boy was not a sports star, but actor Sidney Poitier. However, as he became more fascinated with basketball, he came to admire Julius Erving. The fabulous "Dr. J" had brought his flying acrobatic act to the NBA in the late 1970s. Dr. J's soaring, swooping attacks on the basket had lifted the act of slam dunking to an art form. Along with young basketball players throughout the country, Michael Jordan was inspired to try his own creative, double-pumping jams. He was equally impressed by Dr. J's quiet dignity off the court. Julius Erving gave Jordan a target to shoot for in his basketball career.

Not until his senior year at Laney did Jordan display the same brilliance in basketball that he had shown in baseball. His success came too late to attract national interest. Some of the schools in the nearby Atlantic Coast Conference (ACC) were aware of him, though. University of North Carolina coach Dean Smith was greatly impressed with Jordan at a summer basketball camp that he ran. Smith wished Jordan would hide in a closet for a few months before other schools saw how good he was and started recruiting him. As word spread of Jordan's skill, other ACC recruiters came calling. Jordan listened to the offers. In the end, his parents' concern for education won out. He chose the school that treated him best as a student instead of a basketball recruit. That was Dean Smith's school, the University of North Carolina at Chapel Hill.

How could Dean Smith and Michael Jordan not be smiling? Under Smith's guidance, Jordan became one of college basketball's elite players. Jordan's time at UNC laid the groundwork for him to become arguably the best player in NBA history.

College Star

Jordan did not figure to play much for the powerful North Carolina team in his first year. The Tar Heels had finished second in the National Collegiate Athletic Association (NCAA) championships the previous season. Most of those players were returning for the 1981–82 season. Jordan improved so quickly, though, that he was chosen to fill the spot of the Tar Heels' top scorer Al Wood, who had graduated.

Coach Dean Smith was not sure what to make of this talented six-foot five-inch freshman forward. He cringed at the way Jordan's tongue hung out on his drives to the hoop. Worried that Jordan would bite off his tongue some day, Smith tried to find a special mouthpiece for him. The dentists' best efforts were in vain. Nothing worked.

Smith had better luck curing another of Jordan's problems. The freshman was often frustrated by referees who called him for traveling as he started to drive to the basket. After watching him closely, Smith found that Jordan was not walking with the ball. It only seemed he was because of Jordan's incredible quickness. Coach Smith finally sent a slow-motion videotape of Jordan's move to the ACC referees. That convinced the officials. They stopped blowing the whistle on Jordan.

Jordan spent much of the season getting comfortable with his veteran Tar Heels teammates. He found that he had been playing basketball almost completely on instinct in high school. In order to compete on the next level, he had to learn more about the game of basketball. He was especially weak on defense. Like many high-scoring stars, he so enjoyed putting the ball in the hoop that he paid little attention to stopping the other guy.

The normally aggressive Jordan was also awed by his talented teammates. He often passed up chances to drive into the lane for fear of butting into the territory of North Carolina's veteran front-line stars, James Worthy and Sam Perkins. Yet even with a late-season slump, Jordan finished third on the team in both scoring (13.5 ppg) and rebounding (4.4 rpg). He was voted the ACC Rookie of the Year.

Paced by Worthy and Perkins, North Carolina advanced again to the NCAA Finals. There, Jordan first heard the taunts of "can't win the big one." The critics were saying this about a man Jordan admired, Coach Smith. Since taking over the Tar Heels program in 1961, Smith had put together one of the best records in the

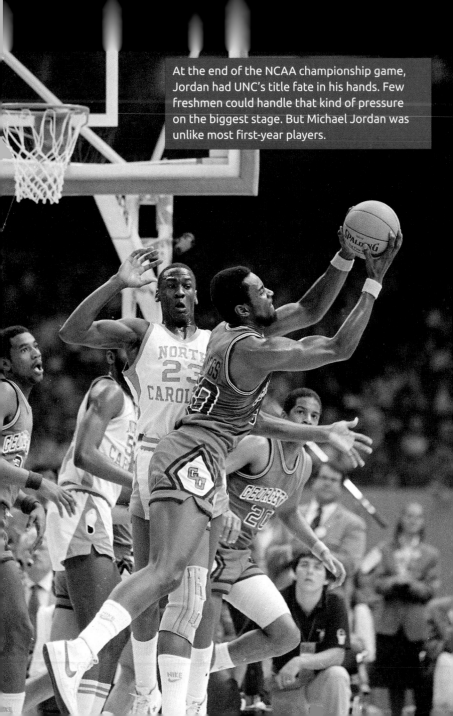

At the end of the NCAA championship game, Jordan had UNC's title fate in his hands. Few freshmen could handle that kind of pressure on the biggest stage. But Michael Jordan was unlike most first-year players.

country. Six times he had taken his team to the NCAA Final Four. Six times he had failed to win.

Jordan and his teammates were determined to win the big one for Coach Smith. Yet they faced an enormous challenge. Waiting for them in the finals was a tough Georgetown University team, led by ferocious freshman center Patrick Ewing. As if the pressure were not enough, they would be playing before what was then the largest basketball crowd in history. More than 61,000 fans crowded into the New Orleans Superdome to watch the action.

After thirty-nine minutes of furious play, only one point separated the teams. Georgetown's Sleepy Floyd then nailed a jump shot to put the Hoyas ahead, 62–61. With thirty-two seconds left, Coach Smith called a timeout to plot strategy for the last shot. James Worthy was the logical choice for the shot. The team's offensive ace led all scorers with 28 points. But if Worthy was covered, Smith expected Jordan to be open. He did not hesitate to pin all his hopes on this unknown freshman. Jordan was to take the shot if it was there.

"I was all kinds of nervous," Jordan says when he heard the strategy. Still, it had been his best game of the season. Jordan had even led the team with 9 rebounds. He felt confident. Sure enough, Georgetown was so concerned about Worthy that the Hoyas left Jordan alone. Michael jumped high in the air from sixteen feet away and launched a shot. It touched nothing but net. Worthy's steal then preserved the 63–62 win and the NCAA championship. Jordan's clutch shot "started everything," according to Michael. It launched him into the national spotlight for the first time.

Jordan posted outstanding statistics his sophomore year. He averaged 20 points and 5.5 rebounds per game. Yet he became a much more complete player. He worked harder on his defense. He improved his on-court decision making. Realizing that he could not always outjump and outrun people, Jordan challenged himself to outthink the other players. Jordan played so hard and so well that he was named College Basketball Player of the Year by *The Sporting News*.

That was when Jordan found out that being a sports idol can turn even the most level head. At the beginning of his junior year, Jordan's play began to slip. Coach Smith had him watch films of his play compared with films from the year before. Jordan could see the difference. He seemed to be trying too hard to show off for the crowd. After settling down to his natural style of play, Jordan matched his sophomore statistics almost exactly. Again he was named *The Sporting News* College Basketball Player of the Year. The Tar Heels went undefeated in the ACC, although they were eliminated from the postseason tournament.

At the end of the 1984 season Jordan faced a tough decision. There was nothing more for him to prove on the college level. If he left college and entered the pro draft, he would command a huge salary. Yet he had been raised to value education. He was holding a B average and was well on his way to earning a degree in geography. Michael discussed the situation with his family and with Coach Smith. He sought advice from James Worthy, who had left school the year before to join the Los Angeles Lakers.

Finally, he made his decision. He would try out for the United States Olympic team that summer and then enter the pro draft.

However, he promised himself he would be back in school at the first opportunity to get his degree.

At the Olympic trials, Jordan showed why he was considered to be the cream of the college crop. His Olympic teammates were impressed not only with Jordan's skill but also with his enthusiasm. Power forward Wayman Tisdale said, "Playing with him was like going to the circus."

Much of the Olympic drama was dampened when the United States' archrival, the Soviet Union, pulled out of the 1984 games in Los Angeles. However, there were still those who were predicting trouble for the United States team. One expert declared that this would be "a weaker team even than the 1972 team" that had lost the gold medal game to the Soviets.

As leader of the United States team in the Olympic Games, Jordan captured millions of new fans. Even those from other ACC schools, who had been rooting against Jordan for three years, now adopted him as their own star. They cheered with every point he scored for the American team.

The Olympic Games turned out nearly as one-sided as a steamroller taking on a carton of eggs. The United States buried its opponents so quickly in eight straight wins that there was little need for Jordan's heroics. USA coach Bobby Knight left Jordan in just long enough to give the world a hint of what he could do. That brief glimpse, during which Jordan averaged 17 points a game, was enough for the Spanish coach. After the United States drubbed Spain 96–65 to win the gold medal, Spain's coach marveled at Jordan's ability to twist and double-pump while in midair. "He's a rubber man. He's not human."

Chapter 4

The Bulls Begin to Win

Jordan may have won over the American public, but there were still doubters among the pro scouts. They pointed out that Jordan, who grew to six-feet six-inches in college, was a bit tall for a guard. Yet he was not quite big enough to play forward. Some scouts figured that Jordan's outside shot was not accurate enough for him to succeed at guard.

Two teams passed up the chance to choose Jordan in the 1984 NBA Draft of college players. The Houston Rockets went for the University of Houston's explosive center, Hakeem Olajuwon. Portland, choosing second, claimed another big man, Kentucky's seven-foot one-inch Sam Bowie.

The Chicago Bulls took Jordan with the third selection

This is Jordan's official photo taken before his rookie season.

of the draft. The Bulls were limping off another in a series of disastrous seasons. They had won 27 and lost 55 in 1983–84. Only once in the past seven years had they even made the playoffs. Bulls fans had grown weary of this dismal show. The team was averaging fewer than 7,000 fans per game.

The Bulls did not expect a rookie to rescue the Chicago team by himself. They could only hope that Jordan might put them back on the road to being respectable again. No one was prepared for what happened. Letting Jordan loose on the NBA courts was like letting an eagle out of a cage!

Jordan admits that he learned a great deal playing in Dean Smith's highly structured system. He held such fondness for his college team that he continued to wear Carolina blue shorts under his extra long Chicago Bulls uniform. The NBA offered the type of basketball that Jordan was meant to play! The twenty-four-second shot clock prevented stalling and forced the pros to keep the pedal to the floor the entire game. There were no zone defenses clogging up the middle to prevent drives to the basket. Star players were free to execute their best moves without waiting for a coach's approval.

All these changes played to Jordan's strengths. He liked to gamble and go for steals. On offense, he liked to try new moves and create new shots. With his quick first step, he could explode past a defender to the basket. If another player stepped in to challenge the shot, Jordan could change his plan in a split second. While hanging in midair, he could pull the ball back down, fake the defender in the air, and then shoot—all before touching the ground. The better the defense, the deeper Jordan would reach into his bag of tricks.

Jordan needed no time to adjust to the pros; he came roaring out of the starting gate. In his second exhibition game, Michael sank 10 of 11 shots from the floor and 12 of 13 from the free throw line. In the third game of the regular season, Jordan broke loose for 22 points in a quarter against the Milwaukee Bucks. He finished the night with 37 points. He squashed any doubts that he could shoot well enough to play guard in the NBA.

It was not the numbers that awed fans as much as the breathtaking way he scored. Jordan was a younger, even springier version of the marvelous Dr. J. He soared so high that he seemed in danger of smashing his head on the backboard. He unleashed the flashiest collection of whirlwind dunks ever seen. There were darting bursts to the rim through three defenders, behind-the-head slams, flying breakaway jams, and dunks where he seemed to walk over the heads of his opponents.

Jordan seemed to defy gravity. His floating leaps made the term "hang time" a part of basketball lingo. Actually, according to the laws of physics, all humans come back to earth at the same rate. Yet Jordan seemed to hang longer because of all the moves he put on while in the air.

Equally refreshing was the joy that Jordan brought to the game. He hustled as though he were the last man on the bench getting his only chance to play. He wore a smile much of the time on court—when his tongue wasn't hanging out. He took time to wink at smaller fans during lulls in the action. Jordan was having the time of his life on the basketball court, and fans were having just as much fun watching him.

The Bulls, who used to draw the smallest road crowds in the league, played to packed houses wherever they went. Jordan was amazed to find opposing fans coming to the game "hoping to see me score 50 points and their team win."

Jordan played every game of the Bulls' 1984–85 season. The man who never put up impressive statistics in college averaged 28.2 points, making him the third highest scorer in the league. He collected 6.5 rebounds and almost 6 assists per game. On defense, his 196 steals ranked fourth in the NBA. Jordan easily beat out Hakeem Olajuwon to win Rookie of the Year honors.

Chicago fans hold up signs in admiration of the greatest player they had ever seen.

The Nike shoe company took advantage of Jordan's popularity by bringing out a new line of basketball shoes. With Jordan's name and face as the shoe's calling card, "Air Jordan" shoes became the most successful product in sports marketing history. Neither Magic Johnson nor Larry Bird, nor even Dr. J, had burst onto the pro scene in such a blaze of glory.

As the 1985–86 season began, Jordan was enjoying life as never before. The shy, unpopular kid had spun a cocoon and come out as America's best-loved sports star. His life was a hurricane of activity. He ran from practices to games, to interviews, to business meetings, to public appearances. Jordan could do no wrong; everything he touched turned to gold.

However, on October 29, 1985, that empire was shaken to its roots. In the third game of the season, Jordan landed awkwardly on his left foot. X-rays showed that he had fractured a bone that supports the ankle and foot.

Except for minor bumps and sprains, Jordan had never been injured. For the first time in his life, he had no place to channel his energy. Like any seriously injured player, he had to fight off doubts about whether his foot would ever be the same. Jordan used the time to finish his college studies at North Carolina. Yet the long weeks of sitting on the sidelines depressed him.

When his foot began healing, Jordan was eager to return to action. However, the Bulls' team doctors were cautious. They recommended that Jordan sit out the season to be safe. That was more than Jordan could stand. Unknown to the Bulls, he began working out with friends in North Carolina. Before long, he was playing basketball two hours a day. He felt so strong that he decided it was ridiculous to sit out. In March, Jordan told the Bulls' management he was ready to play.

The Bulls brought Jordan to Chicago for medical tests. Two of the three doctors who studied the results advised him to sit out the rest of the year to avoid the risk of permanent injury. Jordan's agent agreed. Jordan, however, had reached the end of his patience. "They don't know how my foot feels," he insisted. No one could talk him out of returning to action.

"What Michael is doing makes no sense," complained Bulls owner Jerry Reinsdorf. Frantic with worry, the Bulls pleaded with him to compromise. Jordan agreed to limit his playing time to fourteen minutes a game. Still, Jordan could not hold back his competitive spirit. He hated to sit while his team was losing.

Finally, Jordan chucked aside all caution. While the Bulls' management cringed, the hard-driving, high-flying, tongue-flapping Jordan once again began wrecking NBA defenses. With Jordan leading the charge, Chicago won six of its final nine games to gain a playoff spot.

As the playoff team with the worst record, Chicago drew top-rated Boston as its opening opponent. In Game 1, Jordan lit up Boston's proud defense for 49 points. He topped that by scoring 63 the next game. Although the Celtics won the series easily, they were astounded by the effort of a man who was supposed to be injured. "I just sat there and said, 'Wow!'" declared Boston coach K. C. Jones.

The following season, Jordan picked up where he left off by bombing the New York Knicks for 50 points in the opening game. He continued to rain basketballs on opposing nets throughout the 1986–87 hoops year. In a game against the Atlanta Hawks, Jordan scored 23 points in a row for the Bulls and finished with 61. He ripped through opposing defenses to average 37.1 points per game. Only one person in NBA history, Wilt Chamberlain, had ever posted a higher scoring average.

The Michael Jordan Air Show kept going strong in 1987–88. Jordan led the NBA in both scoring average (35.0) and steals (259). He became the first player ever to win both a scoring title and Defensive Player of the Year award in the same season. Jordan added the league's Most Valuable Player (MVP) award and the All-Star Game MVP award to his trophy case. But even with their star winning almost every possible award, the Bulls

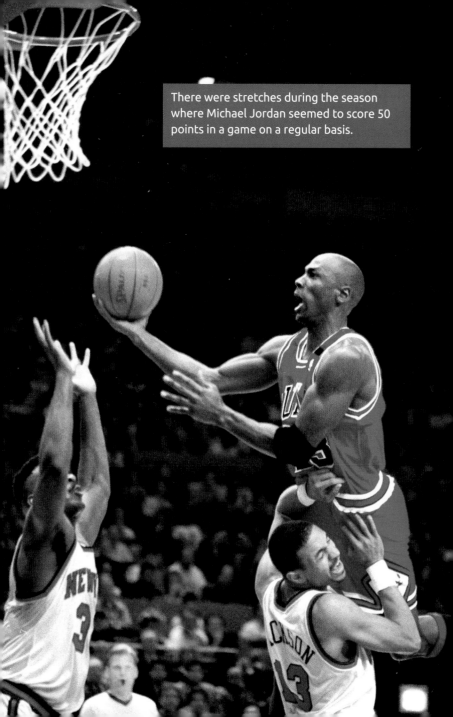

There were stretches during the season where Michael Jordan seemed to score 50 points in a game on a regular basis.

continued to struggle in the playoffs. Jordan could not do it all himself.

Gradually, help arrived. The Bulls drafted power forward Horace Grant and obtained small college wizard Scottie Pippen in a draft-day trade. Center Bill Cartwright also came in a trade. Shooting guard John Paxson signed as a free agent.

While the Bulls steadily improved, Jordan continued to dazzle the league. He won his third straight scoring title in 1988–89 with an average of 32.5 points per game. He set personal bests in rebounds (652), shooting percentage (.538), and assists (650). In the playoffs, Jordan sparked his team to two wins in the first three games of a best-of-five series against favored Cleveland.

Needing one more win to put away Cleveland, Jordan played to exhaustion. He scored 60 points and then drew a last-minute foul as his team clung to a slim lead. If Jordan made the free throws, his team would advance. This time Jordan missed. Cleveland went on to win the game in overtime.

Jordan went into Game 5 with something to prove. This time Cleveland took a 100–99 lead with only three seconds remaining. Everyone in the arena knew who would take the final shot. Cleveland assigned two defenders to him. Six-foot ten-inch leaper Larry Nance hovered between Jordan and the sidelines. Craig Ehlo, a solid defender, tightly guarded Jordan.

Jordan darted free of both defenders just long enough to take the pass. He dribbled twice and jumped. Ehlo jumped with him, set to block the shot. Jordan faked a shot and pulled back the ball out of Ehlo's reach. Just before he fell to the floor,

Jordan walks off the court with his Hall-of-Fame teammate and great friend, Scottie Pippen.

Jordan let the ball fly. He never saw it deflect off the back of the rim and drop through the net! Jordan had won the game.

Chicago's playoff run then came to a halt. The champion Detroit Pistons knocked off the Bulls in the Eastern Conference Finals, four games to two. In 1989–90 the Bulls played better against Detroit. But again Chicago lost in the finals, this time in seven games.

His critics felt that the Bulls inability to win a title was proof that basketball is a team sport and not a one-man game. High scorers never win titles. And Jordan just did not have what it takes to lead his team to a title.

Chapter 5

NBA Champion

Jordan was getting tired of hearing it. "Selfish." "A ball hog." "Not a team player like Magic Johnson and Larry Bird." "He will never win a title."

Publicly, Jordan responded gracefully to the charges. "I'm taking the raps as a challenge to get better and to see that my team gets better," he said. He insisted that he would have no regrets about his career even if he never won a championship. Still, Michael Jordan, the ultimate competitor, wanted that championship in the worst way.

In his seventh season in the NBA, Jordan worked extra hard at helping the Bulls play as a team. "We've all got to dig deeper," he said. "I think I can." Coach Phil Jackson asked Jordan to do

Jordan defends against Lakers guard Magic Johnson. Early in his career, critics claimed Michael Jordan could not win the big game, while Johnson won often. Jordan eventually won his first of six titles against Magic and the Lakers, quieting those critics.

fewer things in 1990–91. Jordan played about two minutes less per game and often let Pippen take charge of the offense.

As a result, Jordan's scoring average dipped to 31.5. It was still enough to win his fifth straight scoring title. More importantly, though, Jordan won his second MVP award and led the Bulls to 61 wins, tops in the league.

It was a determined group of Bulls who stormed into the playoffs that year. The Bulls swept New York in their first series, then battered Philadelphia, four games to one. For the third straight year, they reached the Eastern Conference Finals. For the third straight year, NBA champion Detroit stood in their way of a conference title.

Detroit was the one team that could handle Jordan. Paying little attention to the other Bulls, the Pistons set up three lines of defense against the Bulls star. Joe Dumars, a quick guard, badgered Jordan all over the court. If Jordan slipped past him, defensive ace Dennis Rodman was ready to pick him up. Backing up Rodman was seven-foot shot-blocker John Salley.

This time, however, the Bulls were ready for their archrivals. Jordan spent the first half of each game getting the ball to his teammates for open shots. In the second half he shredded the Pistons defense with his own moves. Chicago stomped the defending champions four straight.

One more hurdle remained before Jordan could shed the loser tag. Magic Johnson, the ultimate team player, had led the Lakers into the finals. The headline matchup of Magic versus Michael only put more pressure on Jordan. Magic wore five championship rings. Jordan wore none.

Game 1 gave Jordan's critics plenty of ammunition. He missed a last-minute shot that would have clinched the win for Chicago. That allowed Jordan's old Tar Heels teammate, Sam Perkins, to win the game with a three-point shot for Los Angeles.

Yet the Bulls star kept his confidence. He could even joke about the heartbreaking outcome. "The wrong North Carolina player made the last shot," he said, with a smile.

As he always did after a personal defeat, Jordan came out blazing in Game 2. He set the tone with a spectacular drive to the middle. When the Lakers big men moved in to block his shot, Jordan switched to his left hand in midair and banked in the layup. Jordan made twelve consecutive shots at one point, as the Bulls blew out the Lakers, 107–88.

In Game 3, Los Angeles streaked to a 13-point second-half lead. Chicago then closed to within two points with time for one last shot. Jordan dribbled the length of the court. He faked Lakers guard Byron Scott and rose high in the air, twelve feet from the basket. Seven-foot Lakers center Vlade Divac challenged the shot. However, Jordan soared over Divac's outstretched arm. The ball swished through the center of the net, sending the game into overtime.

From that moment Chicago took control. The Bulls won the game in overtime and went on to convincing wins in the final two games. Jordan and the Bulls finally had their title! Jordan was the unanimous choice for series MVP. He sat hugging the championship trophy in the locker room with tears streaking his cheeks.

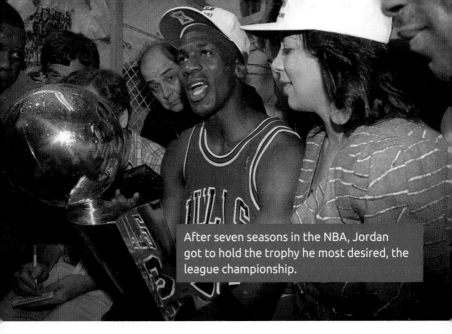

After seven seasons in the NBA, Jordan got to hold the trophy he most desired, the league championship.

"I've never been like this emotionally in public," Jordan said. "But I don't mind. It's been a seven-year struggle."

Now the struggle was over and it was time to reap the rewards. Free from the intense pressure of proving he could win, Jordan soared almost effortlessly through the 1991–92 season. He captured his sixth straight NBA scoring title with a 30.1 average. He easily earned his third MVP award. The Bulls streaked to a 67–15 record, the fourth best mark in league history. Chicago then cruised through the early rounds of the playoffs into the championship series.

Their opponent, the high-powered Portland Trail Blazers, featured their own midair magician in Clyde "the Glide" Drexler. In Game 1 of the NBA Finals, the Blazers backed off Jordan. They concentrated on keeping him away from the basket and dared him to take long three-point shots.

As always, Jordan rose to the challenge. With Portland ahead, 25–17, Jordan went on a wild bombing spree. Launching shots from far behind the three-point line, he scored the next ten points to give his team the lead. By halftime, Jordan had already single-handedly buried the Blazers with 35 points. With Chicago comfortably ahead, he let his teammates do the scoring in the second half and finished with 39 points.

Portland tightened up on Jordan's long-range shooting in Game 2. Jordan responded by slashing and driving for 39 more points, although Portland won the game. Game 3 featured yet another Jordan talent—defense. Led by its star, Chicago hounded Portland into 20 turnovers and captured Game 3.

After three games of being outplayed by Jordan, Portland star Clyde Drexler finally got revenge in Game 4. His crucial steal from Michael gave the Blazers the victory to even the series.

Jordan watchers were ready for some fireworks in Game 5. Nobody ever embarrassed Jordan without paying for it the next game. Sure enough, Jordan sank 14 of 23 shots from the field, and 16 of 19 free throws for 46 points in Chicago's win.

Portland scrapped back in Game 6. The Trail Blazers raced to a double-digit lead in the second half. Then the Bulls, sensing another title, moved in for the kill. After a brief rest, Jordan entered the game in the fourth quarter with Chicago trailing, 81–78. He scored 12 of the Bulls' final 19 points to clinch the 97–93 win and the championship.

Instead of enjoying a well-deserved rest in the off-season, Jordan joined the United States team for the 1992 Summer

Olympic Games. Teaming up with Magic Johnson, Larry Bird, and other NBA stars, Jordan took charge of what many called the best basketball team ever. The "Dream Team," as it was called, destroyed all opposition in the Olympics. They romped to the gold medal, winning their games by an average of nearly 44 points! Even among such skilled teammates, Jordan clearly stood out. He ran the offense, shut down the opponent's best scorer, and scored almost effortlessly.

Shortly after the Olympics ended, it was time to report for the 1992–93 NBA season. The lack of rest took its toll on the Bulls star. The team slumped to a 57–25 mark. Yet even when his tank wasn't quite full, Jordan continued his domination of the record books. His 32.6 scoring average captured an incredible seventh straight scoring title.

The playoffs seemed to recharge Jordan's batteries. He and the Bulls looked sharp in sweeping their opening series against Atlanta and Cleveland. Then they ran into the Knicks, who had won three more games than the Bulls during the regular season.

Playing rugged defense, the Knicks threw the Bulls off stride. After splitting the first two games of the series in New York, they embarrassed Jordan and the Bulls in Game 3. Bumped and battered by the muscular Knicks defenders, Jordan missed 15 of the 18 shots as New York won easily. Furthermore, press reports surfaced that Michael Jordan had a gambling problem. Jordan was so enraged by the reports that he refused to talk to the media.

Embarrass and enrage Michael Jordan? Not a good idea. Jordan came out firing in Game 4. He sank six three-point shots on his way to a 54-point effort. The Knicks never knew what hit them. Overwhelmed by Jordan's play, they dropped the final three games of the series to send Chicago into the finals.

This time Charles Barkley and the Phoenix Suns stood in the way of the Bulls' quest for a third straight title. No team had accomplished the "three-peat" since the Boston Celtics turned the trick back in the 1960s. Yet no team had ever had a player like Jordan.

Michael Jordan is on top of the world after beating the Phoenix Suns to become an NBA champ and Finals MVP for the third year in a row.

Jordan led the Bulls to a fast start with tough defensive play and 31 points in Chicago's opening victory. Barkley, desperate to win his first championship, played his heart out in Game 2, pumping in 48 points. That would have been enough to beat any other team. However, Jordan answered Barkley with 42 points of his own as Chicago won the contest.

Game 3 turned into an exhausting marathon as neither team could hold a lead. Phoenix finally outlasted the Bulls, 129–121, in triple overtime. Jordan scored 44 points, yet was upset with what he called a "subpar" performance. He had taken 45 shots and missed well over half of them.

Michael Jordan upset? Uh-oh. The Suns were in trouble. Jordan took out his frustration in the usual fashion. He put on an offensive basketball clinic. Although Phoenix badly outplayed the rest of the Bulls, Jordan answered every Suns rally. He scored 55 of his team's 111 points in a six-point victory. Suns coach Paul Westphal summed up his team's problem in simple terms. "The big difference was they had Michael and we didn't."

Jordan finished with 41 points despite losing Game 5, and 33 points when the Bulls completed the series victory in Game 6. His 41-point average broke Rick Barry's twenty-six-year-old mark for the championship round.

Michael Jordan stood alone at the top of the basketball world. There seemed to be no one who could challenge his string of MVP awards and scoring championships. And no team could seemingly end the Bulls' three-year reign as champions.

Chapter 6

Levelheaded Leader

As he hugged Chicago's third NBA championship trophy, Jordan seemed to be living a charmed life. He was successful beyond his wildest dreams. His products were selling, earning him millions of dollars every month. He seemed to be living up to his responsibility as a role model to young, adoring fans. In fact, Jordan had so many things going for him that the main question asked of him was, "Is Michael Jordan for real?"

Michael Jordan was for real. The enthusiasm he displayed for the game was genuine. He so loved the game of basketball that he insisted on a "love of the game" clause in his contract. This allowed him to play basketball on playgrounds and streets—whenever and wherever he felt like it.

Sometimes he was a prisoner of his own popularity. The demands on his time and his patience were crushing. He was swamped with requests for appearances. Fans mobbed him wherever he went. Jordan could not attend his local church in Chicago, go shopping, or even see a movie because of the fuss people made over him. Even on the basketball court, Jordan had to skip pregame shooting for fear that his teammates would be bothered by the fuss that followed him everywhere.

Famous people often go into hiding to escape the endless demands of the public. However, Jordan's motto was "Always be positive, respect others, enjoy life." That attitude helped Jordan to accept the frantic pace of the life he was forced to lead. Rather than complaining about his lack of privacy, Jordan tried

A familiar scene for Jordan, being completely surrounded by reporters. Some famous people have trouble dealing will all the attention, but Jordan kept a level head about it.

to satisfy both his own needs and those of his public. When he could no longer go to a restaurant without attracting a mob of fans, Jordan bought his own restaurant. He designed it with a glassed-in room off the ground so that people could see him, while still allowing him privacy to relax with friends and family.

Jordan found the challenge of being a role model to be as intimidating as anything he ever ran into on the basketball court. His popularity put him under tremendous pressure. Everyone makes mistakes now and then. However, Jordan knew he could not afford to slip up. Anything he did would be plastered across newspapers throughout the country.

Jordan was reluctant to set himself up as a role model. He knew that he had faults just like anyone else. He could be moody and demanding, and sometimes got carried away with his competitiveness. Once in a full-court scrimmage with his Bulls teammates, Jordan accused his coach of miscounting the score. Considering that it was only a scrimmage, the point was hardly worth arguing. Yet Jordan became so upset that he walked off the practice court. Jordan's competitiveness also got him into trouble with charges that he was addicted to gambling.

Michael Jordan has accepted the demands of being a role model. "I've been blessed with talent, health, and a loving family," he said. "This is my way of giving something back. It's my dream to continue to help kids long after the ball stops bouncing."

Seventeen-year-old Adam Ference was one of many who found out what Jordan was talking about. Ference was riding a school bus in McKeesport, Pennsylvania, when one of his fellow

Jordan realized many children viewed him as a role model. So he respected all those around him, even referees who he may have felt made a bad call.

riders pulled out a gun. For no proven reason, he shot Ference in the head, and then shot himself. Ference was critically injured.

Following brain surgery, Ference began a slow recovery. Word reached Jordan that he was the high school junior's favorite basketball player. The boy's family hoped that Jordan might send some word of encouragement. Jordan immediately sent Ference the Chicago Bulls shorts he had worn in his last game, autographed.

But that was not all. When the Bulls visited Cleveland, they arranged for Ference to attend the game. While the other Bulls were warming up on the court before the game, Jordan came out of the dressing room to meet Adam. It was not just a case of a star athlete saying a few words to a tongue-tied boy. Jordan was there to listen.

At the end of his time with the boy, Jordan shrugged off the thanks from Adam's grateful parents. "I just want to thank you for giving me the opportunity to meet this young man," said Jordan. That summer Ference was back playing basketball at a Michael Jordan camp. "When I think of Michael Jordan, what I like about him is he goes beyond the court," said Ference.

Many inner-city Chicago boys got the same impression. Jordan stopped to talk with a boy in the street one night after a Bulls game. Jordan gave the boy the Air Jordan shoes that he had worn in the game that night—but only after he made the boy promise to be in school the next day.

The combination of a fierce will to win, enormous talent, and admirable character made Jordan the most popular athlete in the world. Magic Johnson, a legend in his own right, once summed up Jordan's place in the sports world. "Really, there is Michael and then there's everybody else."

While many backyard jump shooters dreamed of being Michael Jordan, there were dangers in being so popular. He earned millions of dollars every month. Experts called him the best basketball player ever. People fawned all over him wherever he went. How could anyone keep that from going to his head?

Jordan took a levelheaded approach to his stardom. He remembered that hard work got him where he was. Anyone who has seen Jordan soar high above the basket and twist his body into an impossible position knows that Jordan is blessed with wonderful athletic skill. Yet Jordan made the most of that skill with relentless practicing. Even after he reached the top, Jordan continued to awe his coaches with his need to drive himself to exhaustion in practices.

Jordan also took a cautious approach to his finances. Instead of spending madly or leaving his financial decisions to others, Jordan saw business management as yet another challenge. The world of business "took some getting used to," Jordan said. "But now I enjoy the off-court stuff. I'm learning all the time." His ability to deal comfortably with all kinds of people served him well. His role as spokesman for products from breakfast food to shoes made him far more money than he earned from the Bulls.

Jordan avoided the temptation of a party life. He steered clear of alcohol and drugs. He settled down to a family life by marrying Juanita Vanoy in 1990. He declared that their three children were the most important responsibilities of his life. The quiet, productive habits he had developed as a youngster stayed with him. For a time, Jordan, the wealthy superstar, continued to do his own housework and mend his own clothes.

Most importantly, Jordan stayed close with the friends and family he trusted. "They would let me know if I was starting to get bigheaded," he said.

Yet tragedy can strike even the most stable, comfortable, successful life. In the summer of 1993, Jordan's father, James, suddenly disappeared. After three weeks of worrying, the Jordans' worst fears were confirmed. James Jordan was found shot to death near McCall, South Carolina. Two youths were charged with killing Jordan and stealing his automobile.

Instantly, Michael Jordan's world was shattered. Without his closest friend and advisor to share his triumphs and disappointments, the world seemed empty. Jordan realized that after winning so many championships and scoring awards, he had nothing left to prove to anyone. The grind of long practices and traveling around the country lost its appeal. The harsh glare of news cameras and the barking of reporters became unbearable.

On October 6, 1993, just before the start of the new basketball season, Jordan made the announcement that threw Chicago fans into shock. He was retiring from basketball. Though he was only thirty years old, and at the peak of his game, he was walking away.

"I'm never coming back to play basketball," he told his disbelieving audience. "Not in this lifetime."

Chapter 7

Back to Being the Best

Even more bewildering than Jordan's sudden retirement was the news of what Jordan planned to do with his time. The basketball star signed a contract with the Chicago White Sox.

Critics warned that the whole thing was just a publicity stunt. The White Sox obviously were trying to stir up fan interest in their team. After all, Jordan had not played baseball since high school. Baseball requires precise timing and many years of practice. Nobody started a baseball career at the age of thirty!

Furthermore, Jordan was used to being the king of his sport, earning millions of dollars and warehouses full of awards. If he was serious about a pro career, he would have to start out in the minor leagues. Instead of flying first class to games, he would have to ride the team bus, and dress in run-down locker rooms. He would make less money for the season than he made in a single game as a Bull.

Jordan, however, insisted that this was no joke. His reasons were personal and intense. First, James Jordan had loved baseball. Before Michael showed such a flair for basketball, James had hoped that Michael would develop into a major-league ballplayer. Jordan was doing this for his dad. Secondly, he was doing it for himself. Having run out of challenges on the basketball court, Jordan set out to climb a mountain of a challenge on the baseball diamond.

Jordan attacked his new career with his usual fierce determination. He spent hours each day in the batting cage and on the field. He sought advice from coaches and instructors and did whatever they asked of him. Despite the distractions of the media circus surrounding his effort, Jordan did his best to fit in with his new teammates. When he joined Chicago's AA minor-league team, the Birmingham Barons, he asked for no special treatment. In the words of one teammate, "He was like anybody else on the team. He was trying to get to the same place we're trying to get to."

Jordan's baseball performance proved that he was no superman. Although he showed flashes of his tremendous natural coordination, his inexperience showed both in the field and at the plate. Jordan batted only .202 for Birmingham in 1994. Despite being much larger than the average baseball player, he connected on only three home runs.

Jordan is shown taking batting practice for the Chicago White Sox during spring training in 1994.

Jordan insisted that success was not the important thing in his baseball tryout. All that mattered was that he gave his best effort. Yet Jordan's pride and his hotly competitive nature took a severe battering from his lack of success.

One night his Birmingham team was playing in a half-empty stadium in Memphis, Tennessee. Birmingham trailed in the bottom of the ninth. When two batters made outs, the team's final hopes rested on Jordan. Looking gangly in his baseball uniform, the six-foot six-inch outfielder flailed awkwardly at a pitch for strike three. The game was over.

The Memphis team had scheduled a fireworks display for after the game. As the contest had run late, the lights were immediately turned out so the show could begin. Michael Jordan never moved after striking out. He stood in the batters box in the darkness, staring at the pitcher's mound. At that moment the thrill of a game-winning shot or the thunderous applause that came with a trophy presentation seemed light-years away.

Meanwhile, both the Chicago Bulls and the NBA were struggling with the loss of their superstar. Without Jordan, the three-time defending champions were not even considered title contenders. The Bulls bowed out of the 1994 playoffs, losing to the Knicks in an early round. The NBA could offer nothing to replace the excitement that Jordan provided. The championship series between the Houston Rockets and the New York Knicks featured bruising defenses. Their low-scoring contests resembled a tug-of-war more than a basketball game.

Fans lost interest. Television ratings for pro basketball dropped 31 percent in one year.

As the NBA drifted through its second Jordan-less season, Jordan himself kept working at his new game. He reported to the White Sox spring training camp in February 1995, ready to go back to work. However, a problem developed. The major-league ballplayers were on strike. If Jordan wanted to continue his baseball quest, he would have to cross the ballplayers' picket lines.

Jordan refused, knowing that would hurt the players' cause. He also knew that at his age he could not afford to waste a year doing nothing. Since there seemed to be no end in sight to the baseball strike, Jordan turned his attention back to basketball. After eighteen months away from the sport, Jordan held a different attitude. His ego had taken a beating as he repeatedly floundered against more experienced baseball players. Both the NBA and the Bulls needed him desperately. There were doubts that, after a long layoff, Jordan could return to his former level as a basketball player. The challenge was back. On March 18, 1995, Jordan thrilled Chicago Bulls fans by announcing he was returning.

Jordan's plan was to use what remained of the regular season as a tune-up. "The regular season is garbage," he commented privately. In fact, he was relieved that he had missed most of it. Playoffs were the exciting time of basketball. Jordan aimed to play himself back into shape in time to make a run at the championship.

The "Second Coming of Jordan" dominated sports headlines

in March. Showing signs of the long layoff, Michael scored only 19 points in his first game, against Indiana. He looked rusty when the Orlando Magic whipped the Bulls later that week. Observers whispered that Jordan had lost some of his skills.

Then, on March 25, Jordan popped in a last-second jump shot to beat the Atlanta Hawks. Three days later, the Jordan of old resurfaced at Madison Square Garden in New York. Jordan ripped through the Knicks to score 55 points in a 113–111 victory. It had taken Jordan less than two weeks to regain his spot as the NBA's best scorer.

With Jordan back on board, the Bulls recovered from a slow start. Even though Chicago finished with only a 47–35 record, many experts predicted the team could win the championship. After all, the Bulls had Michael Jordan and no one else did.

Jordan justified their faith in Game 1 of the playoffs against the Charlotte Hornets. He scored 48 points, including 10 in overtime, to clinch the victory. "I felt like a shark in the water and I saw blood and I had to attack," he explained. The Bulls went on to dispose of the Hornets, moving on to challenge the Orlando Magic.

There, Jordan and the Bulls ran smack into reality. The brash young Magic, led by Shaquille O'Neal and Penny Hardaway, were fresher and stronger. Jordan seemed a step slow at times, and lacked his usual confidence. His woeful first game performance caused him to ditch his new No. 45 in favor of the old 23. Yet a change of numbers could not change the fact that Jordan had been away from basketball for eighteen months. He

Jordan gave an all-out effort to get his team a championship after his year and a half absence. But the Orlando Magic was just too much for the Bulls in the playoffs.

failed to come through at crucial times and Orlando took the series, four games to two.

Never before had Michael Jordan been shown up in a basketball series. He spent the off-season in brutal workouts, determined to erase the humiliation. Jordan entered the 1995–96 season as a man on a mission. As he later said, "I wanted to prove I could still play this game." He took special exception to young college stars looking to take over his position as the game's top star. When Philadelphia rookie Jerry Stackhouse bragged about how easy the NBA was, Jordan took him to school. He buried Stackhouse under a 48-point barrage.

Winning, however, was most important. Jordan did not mind his new teammate Dennis Rodman stealing all the attention with his outrageous behavior. As long as Rodman's rebounding and defense helped the Bulls win, that was what mattered.

In a history-making season, Jordan left no doubt that he could still play. He averaged 30.4 points a game to beat Hakeem Olajuwon for a record eighth scoring championship. Answering critics who said he had lost his quickness, Jordan finished third in the NBA in steals. Pushed by Jordan's quest for the title, the Bulls overwhelmed their league opponents. Chicago posted the best record in NBA history, winning 72 games and losing only 10.

Still, as Jordan noted, none of those honors would mean a thing without the championship. Chicago brushed off its early playoff opponents, Charlotte and New York, with little difficulty. That gave them a shot at the team that Jordan had been aiming for all year—the Orlando Magic.

Orlando was one of the favorites to win the NBA title. However, even they could not stand up against the fury of Michael Jordan on a mission. Jordan sparked his team to a stunning 121–83 Game 1 blowout.

With their pride wounded, the Magic roared back in Game 2. They sprinted out to an 18-point second half lead. At that point, Jordan again proved that defense was as important a part of his game as offense. He and his teammates played such fierce defense that the Magic fell apart. The Bulls repeatedly stole the ball and forced bad passes. A seemingly easy Orlando victory turned into a shocking 93–88 defeat.

In Game 3 the Bulls again applied the defensive pressure. The Magic could score only 10 points in the final quarter and 67 for the game. Chicago won easily. Jordan then put the finishing touches on the shell-shocked Magic. He pumped in 45 points as the Bulls got their revenge on Orlando with a four-game sweep.

That brought Chicago to the NBA Finals against the Seattle SuperSonics. Jordan and the Bulls struggled on offense. Their defense helped them pull out victories in the first two games in Chicago. Jordan knew that Game 3 was the key to the series. Seattle would be playing for pride in front of their cheering fans. If they won, they could turn the series around.

Jordan was determined to discourage the Sonics and their fans early in the game. He personally quieted the crowd by scoring 27 points in the first half. The Sonics never recovered from Jordan's barrage and they staggered to an embarrassing defeat.

The Sonics recovered to win the next two games. Then in Game 6, Jordan had one of his worst shooting days in a championship series. He made only 5 of 19 shots. As Jordan said afterward, "Our shooting has been up and down. But our defense has never deserted us." Dennis Rodman, Scottie Pippen, and the rest of the Bulls joined Jordan in shutting down the Sonics and gaining the victory.

Although it was his fourth NBA title in six years, this one meant so much to Jordan that he wept on the floor of the training room. "It was hard," he said. "But winning a championship is supposed to be hard."

For the fourth time in four NBA Finals appearances, Jordan was named the championship MVP. *Sport* magazine named him the top athlete of the last half century.

The Bulls rewarded Jordan by signing him to an astounding $25 million one-year contract for the 1996–97 season. The Bulls breezed through the regular season, and then eliminated the Utah Jazz in the NBA Finals in six games. Jordan then signed a contract for the 1997–98 season worth over $30 million. Jordan and the Bulls went on to win their third straight NBA title, Chicago's second 3-peat in the Jordan era. He finished the 1997–98 season by winning the NBA MVP, the NBA All-Star Game MVP, and the NBA Finals MVP awards.

The 1998–99 season was delayed because of a lockout. Jordan decided to retire for the second time prior to the start of the shortened season.

Jordan shows off his sixth NBA Finals MVP trophy after the Bulls successfully completed their run at a second three-peat.

In 2000, Michael Jordan became the president and partial owner of the Washington Wizards. The Wizards had only made the playoffs once in the previous twelve years. With Jordan running things, Wizards fans hoped for a change. Instead, the team won just 19 games during his first full season in the front office.

To help the product on the court, Jordan came out of retirement for a second time before the 2001 season. He was now thirty-eight years old and had not played in over three full seasons. Still, Jordan averaged over 20 points per game in the two seasons he played for Washington. But the Wizards were not very good, and Jordan retired for the final time. He was then fired from his job as President of Basketball Operations.

In 2005, Jordan returned to the NBA when he became became partial owner of the Charlotte Bobcats. He would become majority owner in 2010. His marriage to Juanita Vanoy

Jordan gives his Naismith Memorial Basketball Hall of Fame induction speech on September 11, 2009.

ended in 2006, but Jordan stayed involved in his children's lives. He watched both his sons play college basketball, and his daughter go off to college as well. In 2011, Jordan became engaged to longtime girlfriend, model Yvette Prieto.

Jordan took his rightful place in the Naismith Memorial Basketball Hall of Fame in 2009. During his enshrinement speech, Jordan had this to say about basketball:

> *It has provided me with a platform to share my passion with millions in a way I neither expected nor could have imagined in my career. I hope that it's given the millions of people that I've touched the optimism and the desire to achieve their goals through hard work, perseverance, and positive attitude. Although I'm recognized with this tremendous honor of being in the Basketball Hall of Fame, I don't look at this moment as a defining end to my relationship with the game of basketball. It's simply a continuation of something that I started a long time ago. One day you might look up and see me playing the game at 50. (laughs) Oh, don't laugh. Never say never. Because limits, like fears, are often just an illusion. Thank you very much. Looking forward to it.*

The fans came to catch the spirit and the artistry that Jordan brought to the game. Air Jordan is so much fun that even veterans admitted they sometimes found themselves standing and watching.

Long after Jordan hung up his last pair of Air Jordan shoes, his legend has remained. It has not been captured by statistics or numbers of championships. Rather, the memories of Jordan will echo the words of one admiring opponent who tried to guard him: "All I saw were the bottoms of his shoes."

Career Statistics

Season	Team	G	FG%	REB	AST	STL	BLK	PTS	PPG
1984-85	Chicago	82	.515	534	481	196	69	2,313	28.2
1985-86	Chicago	18	.457	64	53	37	21	408	22.7
1986-87	Chicago	82	.482	430	377	236	125	3,041	37.1
1987-88	Chicago	82	.535	449	485	259	131	2,868	35.0
1988-89	Chicago	81	.538	652	650	234	65	2,633	32.5
1989-90	Chicago	82	.526	565	519	227	54	2,753	33.6
1990-91	Chicago	82	.539	492	453	223	83	2,580	31.5
1991-92	Chicago	80	.519	511	489	182	75	2,404	30.1
1992-93	Chicago	78	.495	522	428	221	61	2,541	32.6
1993-94	RETIRED								
1994-95	Chicago	17	.411	117	90	30	13	457	26.9
1995-96	Chicago	82	.495	543	352	180	42	2,491	30.4
1996-97	Chicago	82	.486	482	352	140	44	2,431	29.6
1997-98	Chicago	82	.465	475	283	141	45	2,357	28.7
1998-99	RETIRED								
1999-2000	RETIRED								
2000-01	RETIRED								
2001-02	Washington	60	.416	339	310	85	26	1,375	22.9
2002-03	Washington	82	.445	497	311	123	39	1,640	20.0
	TOTAL	1,072	.497	6,672	5,633	2,514	893	32,292	30.1

G = Games   FG% = Field Goal Percentage   REB = Rebounds   AST = Assists
STL = Steals   BLK = Blocks   PTS = Points   PPG = Points per game

More Info

Contact Michael Jordan

Mr. Michael Jordan
c/o Charlotte Bobcats
Time Warner Cable Arena
333 East Trade Street
Charlotte, NC 28202

Facebook: http://www.facebook.com/MichaelJordan

On the Internet At:

<http://www.nba.com/history/players/jordan_stats.html>

Index